♩♩♩

SELF PUBLISH USING KDP AND
INTRODUCTION TO ACX-AUDIBLE
(a primer)

Cover art is a painting of St. Matthew by
Caravaggio, circa 1585 AD

Author: John Julius Candelaria

About the author: Born in Albuquerque, New Mexico. Graduated from University of Albuquerque, earning a BA with majors in Psychology and Art.

without the written permission of the author. You may utilize the examples in this book for reference and must use your own data within the context of all examples.

Other books by John Julius Candelaria:

Sara

Aminah

Sparrow

Machine

Blue Seagull

Proxima Centauri

Dementia (an essay)

Johnny and the Spider

Inspiration, Population 66

Anthology of personal ads

Humanity, version1.1 (an essay)

A discussion with my Goldfish, Electra, about god

This primer is dedicated to writers

An author attempts to control a reader's attention, also tries to present the story in an understanding way. However, the author cannot over-ride a reader's innate attention span or a reader's comprehension ability. As a reader's eyes come upon each written word they silently speak the word. How the reader articulates their speech "aloud" to the world is how a reader "listens" to his or her self reading.

CONTENTS:

FOREWORD

Today, there are three types of book formats a reader can enjoy:

1: Traditional paperbacks or hard cover books.

2: E-books: They are digital files of a complete book anyone can download from an E-book provider like Amazon and read on a Kindle device, or any computer or smartphone with an appropriate app. I personally utilize the "Sali" voice feature of my Kindle to read to me whenever I do not care to read. Only a Kindle device is capable of reading a Kindle E-book aloud due to Kindle-propriety.

3: Audio books: Those books are also digital but utilize a human voice rather than a synthesized voice to read to you. Audio books can be purchased and downloaded from a company like Audible.

Pairing a smartphone with an Audible app to your vehicle's entertainment system allows you to enjoy listening to a book while you drive.

Self-publishing companies such as KDP and ACX do not charge fees to accept your E-book, paperback or Audio-book files to make them available to the public for sale. Those companies earn revenues from sales of audio books and pay royalties to you.

Audio-book dictation software such as "Audacity" is free; allowing, you to dictate your book, then produce and publish it using Amazon's ACX. Thereupon, your audio book will be available at Audible and I-Tunes.

So, is a self-published book of any format different than books published by publishing companies?

No. Publishing houses use the same software programs that are available to the public for preparing a book to send the book-file to a printing company for final book distribution.

Once a book is available to the public it does not matter to any reader if a major publishing house published your book, or if "you" self-published it. Nor does an audiobook listener care who produced the audiobook so long as the reading and listening experience is pleasurable.

Technology has brought much change concerning book publishing. No longer is it necessary to have publishing companies subjectively accept your book manuscript before your book is available to the masses. Today's technology allows a person to write and illustrate a book on their home computer and then utilize a "free" self-publishing internet site to produce and sell your book for the world to read or listen to it; whence you shall earn royalties from sales of your books.

Regarding royalties: When I enlisted in Amazon's KDP in 2015 (which was Createspace at that time) I was required to fill out certain tax form documents since I would be receiving royalty income from Amazon and Audible. Additionally, I had to complete a form with my bank routing number because Amazon pays royalties direct to my bank. At year's end I receive a 1099 from Amazon for when I prepare my personal IRS State tax returns. I post Amazon and Audible royalties under "miscellaneous income" on my IRS tax return.

•

My desire to write a book manifested when I first listened to my mother read a book to me while I was in my crib. Yes, our memories are created at a very early age. But it was not until 2015 when I wrote a book and self-published it using Amazon's free Kindle Direct Publishing (KDP) internet site. I subsequently wrote 11 more books using Amazon's KPD, and narrated 2 audio-books using ACX-

Audible. My self-published audio books using ACX-Audible will be discussed in the final chapter of this Primer.

Do not write your book, expecting become rich by it. The only reason I write books is for the love of it. Do I hope one of my books will be a hit someday and perhaps a movie will come of it? No. I write for pleasure, not for wishful longings.

It is of great importance for anyone reading this primer to know the "key word" is primer. This instructional book is "not" a full-blown classroom.

I personally learn from examples; therefore, this primer is presented in that manner. I encourage you to indulge yourself in as much self-publishing informational material as you can absorb while reading this primer. After you enroll in KDP, I also encourage you to read KDP's resource material on their web site. If you diligently follow the forthcoming instructions, your book covers and interior manuscript "will" pass KDP's requirements. Then, about 24 hours after you upload your book files, your E-book and paperback will be displayed and for sale on Amazon.

For this primer; my book examples are for a 6"X9" 40-page book with cream paper, and without interior illustrations. If you already have a written manuscript that is longer or shorter than 40 pages, simply cut or cut-and-paste portions of your manuscript so the book is 40 pages. We are preparing a "test" using examples for you to gain experience and successfully pass KDP's requirements. Once your "test" book using my examples has been successfully uploaded, you can remove it. With experience gained, you are then free to write a book of any length.

Self-publishing may appear daunting; but so goes any complex endeavor leading to a great reward.

Books are eternal, thus I prepared this primer to assist anyone wishing to leave something of their self behind besides dust when their journey through this life concludes.

ITEMS REQUIRED

If your intention is to only write an E-book you need a computer with a word processor such as Word. Your book cover will require Photoshop to create it. KDP offers bookcover pre-designed templates, also manuscript templates. This book will not explain their usage because this primer is designed to build a book from scratch.

You should have some working knowledge about using Photoshop to design your book covers. However, this primer is built around "examples"; therefore, deep knowledge of Photoshop is not essential. Youtube and other resources offer a great deal of assistance for using Photoshop.

All 12 of my books utilized Windows7, Word 2003, Photo Shop 6 and Adobe Acrobat. At KDP; e-books and e-book covers do not require PDF conversion from jpegs or word documents, but paperback manuscripts and book covers do. Hence, Acrobat, or a low-priced program like "Nuance PDF Create" is required for converting Word docs to PDF. Photoshop has built-in PDF conversion for illustrations.

Kindle Direct Publish (KDP) has strict requirements regarding properly preparing an entire E-book or paperback before the book file is accepted for publishing and offered for sale.

Paper-back book cover content must have precise placement on covers before a completed book file is sent from KDP to a printing facility to physically build the book. To assist you in meeting those precise cover requirements I employ KDP's "cover templates" that were created for specific page count. In this primer; my book is 40 pages, so I downloaded KDP's 40 page cover template and then placed my Photoshop created cover onto the skeleton template; thus assuring KDP's cover dimension restrictions would be met. KDP's cover skeleton template visually depicts bleed, trim and spine dimensions to assist you with exact placement of your Photoshop cover creation. Later, your developed book-cover creation skills shall not need the KDP cover-template.

KDP's multiple-step approval process during upload is automated. If interior formatting errors are found, they can be fixed using Word. Book-cover errors are corrected using Photo Shop. Common book-cover errors are improper "image size" which is a matter of entering correct values in Photoshop "image size." Another common error is: cover content spilling over book edges where the book-printer trims the book. Those errors can be more difficult to fix, so make certain to follow "trim guides" on KDP's cover-template. "Bleed" means cover content bleeds onto the areas where the book-printer trims your book cover; if you adhere to proper "trim" allowance, bleed errors will not be an issue. Do not be overly concerned with "bleed"; just make certain to not over-run book-cover content beyond cover-template "trim guides." A book-cover dimensional math formula for specific book size and page count will be presented later in this primer for determining proper trim and spine width in the event you are adept at using Photoshop and prefer not to use the KDP cover template; or, will use the cover-template only as a visual aid.

Following my "example illustrations" should allow you to pass KDP's quality checks during uploading by greatly reducing formatting and cover errors. Using my learn-by-example approach may provide you with understanding about what causes self-publishing errors.

Humans make errors. A human prepared this primer, so do not expect perfection. I thus encourage you to utilize other sources to reach your self-publishing goals. When I prepared my first book I had to weave through a myriad of resources to piece together a workable method to successfully pass KDP and ACX quality checks before my efforts were acceptable. I admittedly engaged in many phone calls with KDP and ACX support staff before I mastered self-publishing. The Amazon support team is excellent.

Please be aware this primer was built around Word 2003 and Photoshop-6. All examples here are illustrations using those versions. If you are using a different version of Word and Photoshop you must take that into account and be prepared to make adjustments.

I used normal Times New Roman font size 12 for the bulk of my book interior. I utilized other fonts and sizes for Photoshop. In Word, I chose 150% zoom setting to write my book and avoid visual errors. I also box-checked "Blue background" in Word tools, options, general options to prepare my book because a white "working" background seemed too stark for my eyes. Those personal selections are strictly subjective.

Please make your preferential selections in Word tools, options: I checked and unchecked several box-options under all the tabs which are my subjective preferences. Under tools, auto correct, I unchecked every option under every tab because I prefer Word to not make "correction" decisions as I type. There are many more other subjective choices in tools, options which the writer can make. Experiment freely with Word options until you are comfortable with what Word can and cannot do.

Be aware, Word's "defaults" may be okay, but are not always in your best interest. Also note: even seasoned Word and Photoshop users often stumble. Microsoft provides answers and resolves for many issues you may encounter using Word. Adobe is not much help for supporting Photoshop, but Youtube and other resources resolve Photoshop issues, and Word concerns.

Although Youtube and various "help" forums are wonderful resources for solving issues using Word and Photoshop; be careful when reading, watching and listening to people on the internet attempting to provide solutions to issues you may encounter while using Word and Photoshop. Many internet sources offering help are far from expert and may lead you astray. Some internet resources merely wish to demonstrate how smart they are. Toward that self-empowering interest, they will lead you absolutely nowhere. However, there are indeed sincerely helpful resources on the internet that benefit you.

PREPARING YOUR BOOK INTERIOR

Note: Some picture "examples" in this exercise were intentionally skewed for laying out the examples to be more clearly visual. Your actual results from following my examples will not be skewed.

Open Word, click on View and select Print Layout.

Go to File, then Page Setup and under Margins-tab, do:

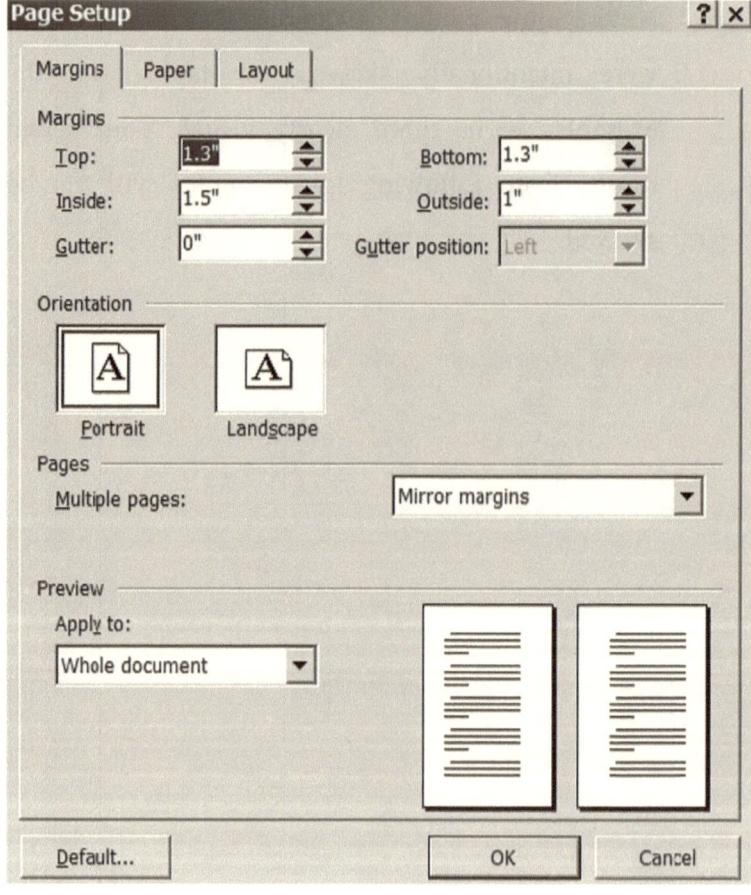

Then go to Paper-tab and do:

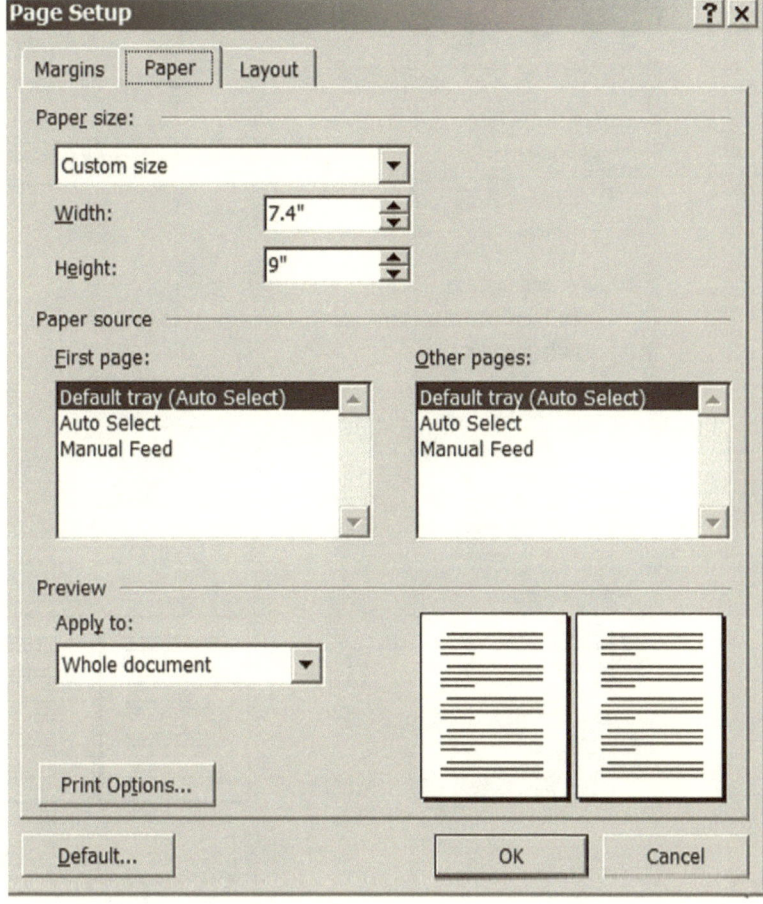

Select Layout tab and do:

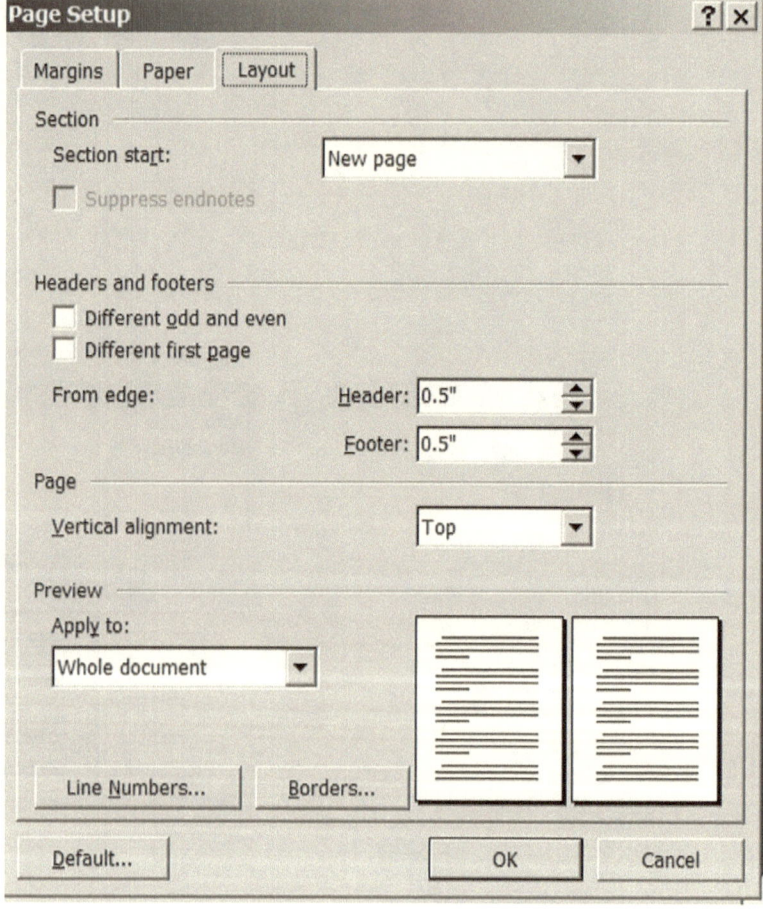

Next click on Format, then do:

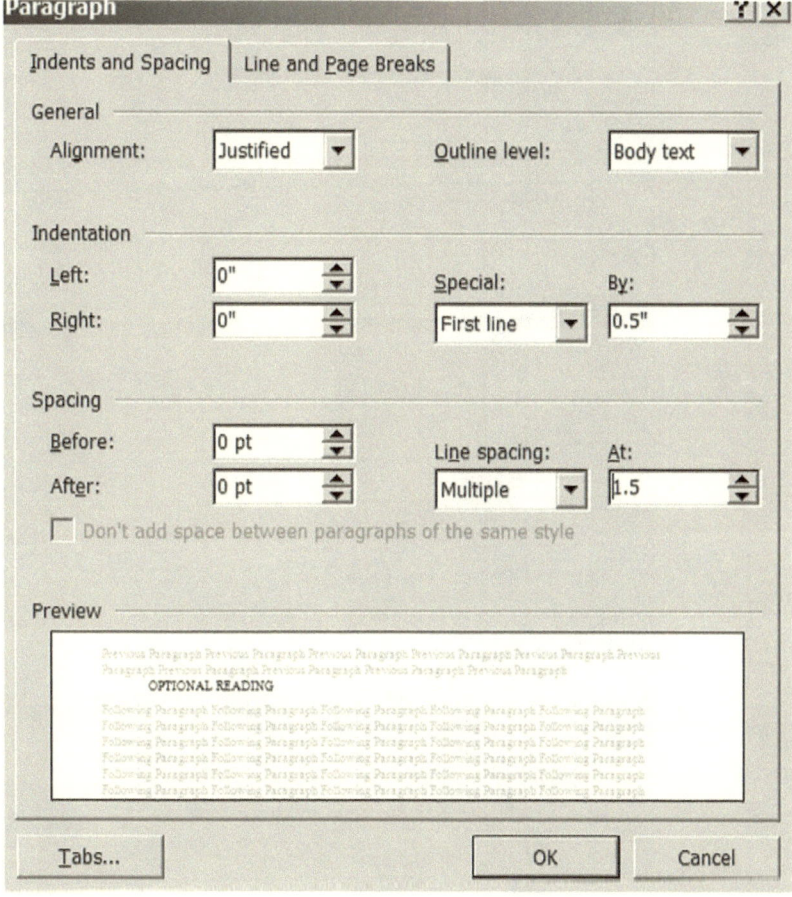

Select Line and page breaks-tab then do:

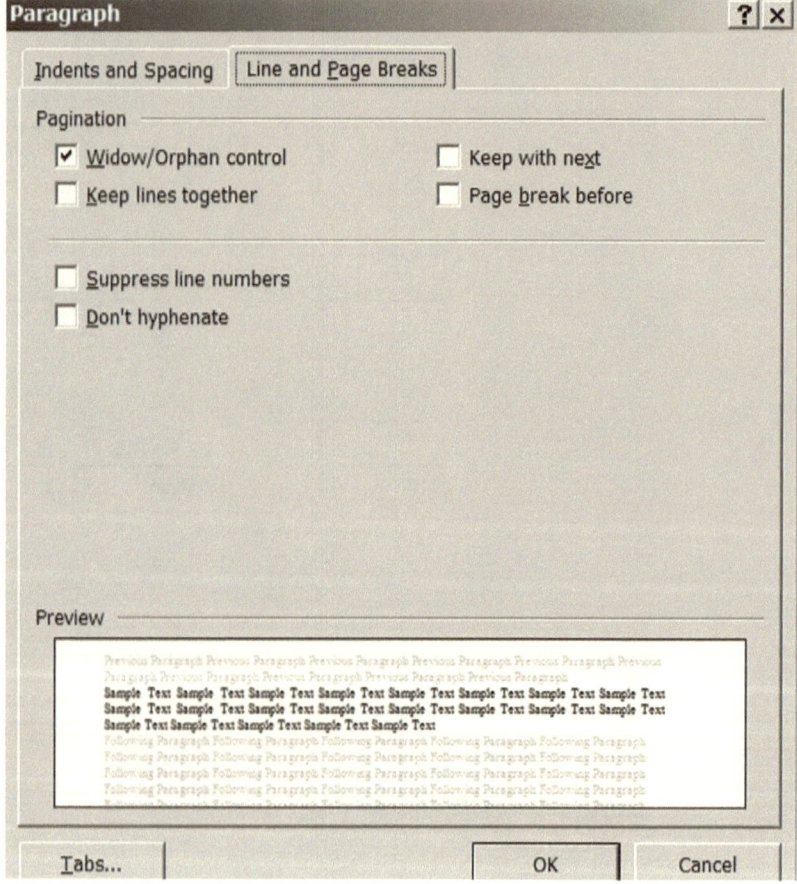

Next: Select Format, and click on Styles and Formatting. The settings should appear as below

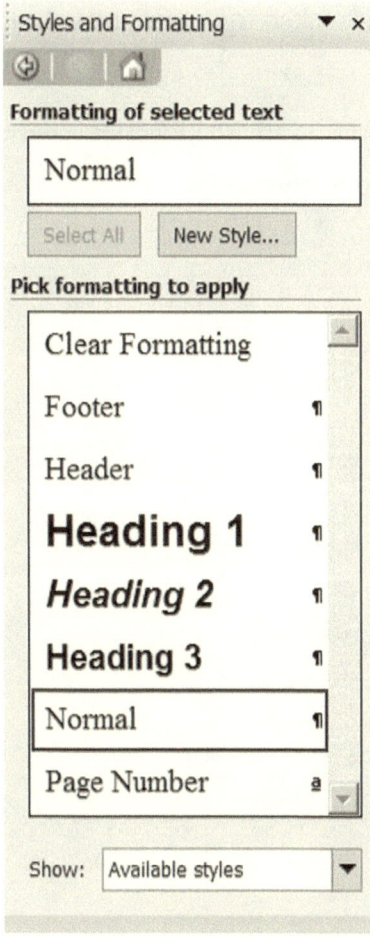

Next step is to type the book title on the first page of your book, then center the title and place it to appear symmetrical on the page as in the following example (the title page is taken from this primer).

Use "page breaks" wisely to keep certain page content independent from others pages.

Example

SELF PUBLISH USING
KDP AND AUDIBLE
(a primer)

Next step is to set "page numbering." Click on "Insert" and choose Page numbers, then do:

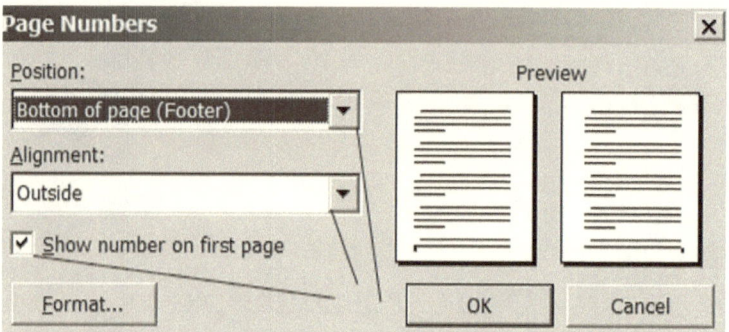

You may of course choose to have page-numbering the way you wish.

Next step is to build your author page with a selfie and add remarks regarding your book. KDP requires the photo file is at least 300 resolution. My photos and illustrations are 500 resolution for better clarity. Larger resolution is overkill and requires long upload times.

Below is an example of author's selfie:

Photoshop settings for the author's selfie above are on the following page:

Note "constrain" box is checked in this instance to best suit photo's balance, but the "constrain" box is typically unchecked in other examples.

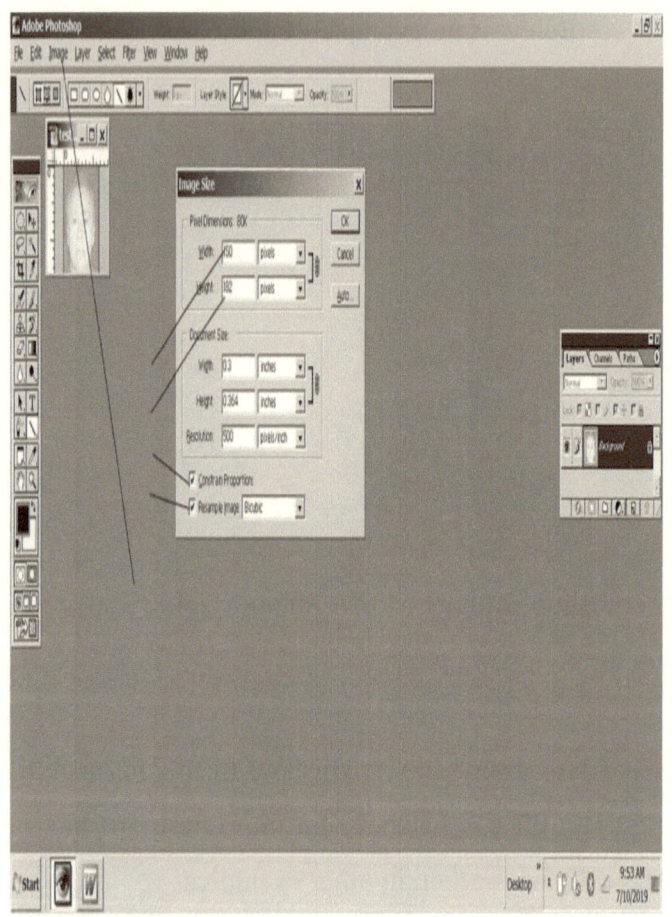

On the following two pages I show the inserted author's photo with author's personal info, also details the author wished to address concerning his book. These two pages of examples can serve as "author-detail" templates for most books.

Also note in the following examples: format settings are "Center" aligned for the photo, also right-space tweaking applied for the author's name to be properly aligned under the selfie. The "About author" section is "justified" and 1.5 double spaced:

Example

Author: John Julius Candelaria

About the author: Born in Albuquerque, New Mexico. Graduated from University of Albuquerque, earning a BA with majors in Psychology and Art.

This book, "Your Title," is a work of fiction. The story, names, characters, businesses, organizations, places, events, and any incidents are either the product of the author's imagination or are used fictitiously. If certain institutions, agencies, or entities are mentioned the characters involved in them are wholly imaginary. Any resemblance to actual persons living or dead, events, or locales is strictly coincidental.

Next step will be to prepare a dedication page and then setup an inscription page.

Examples are presented on the following two pages.

Note: formatting is "Center" alignment and "Align left" with 1.5 line spacing. The typed passages are fitted symmetrically on the pages.

Remember to "page break" each of the following pages so they stand independently:

Example

This book is dedicated to readers

Example

An author attempts to control a reader's attention, also tries to present the story in an understanding way. However, the author cannot over-ride a reader's innate attention span or a reader's comprehension ability. As a reader's eyes come upon each written word they silently speak the word. How the reader articulates their speech "aloud" to the world is how a reader "listens" to his or her self reading.

Next step is to prepare a "Contents" page as in the following page.

Note: formatting is "Center" alignment.

CONTENTS:

Next step is a "Foreword" or "Preface" page. Formatting will be "Center" alignment and 1.5 line spacing.

Type whatever you wish as a prelude to your story. An example of a "Preface" page is not presented here because it follows previous layout examples.

Next step is to type your story. Choose "Justified" alignment and then click on Format, paragraph. My suggestions for paragraph formatting your story are depicted on the following two pages:

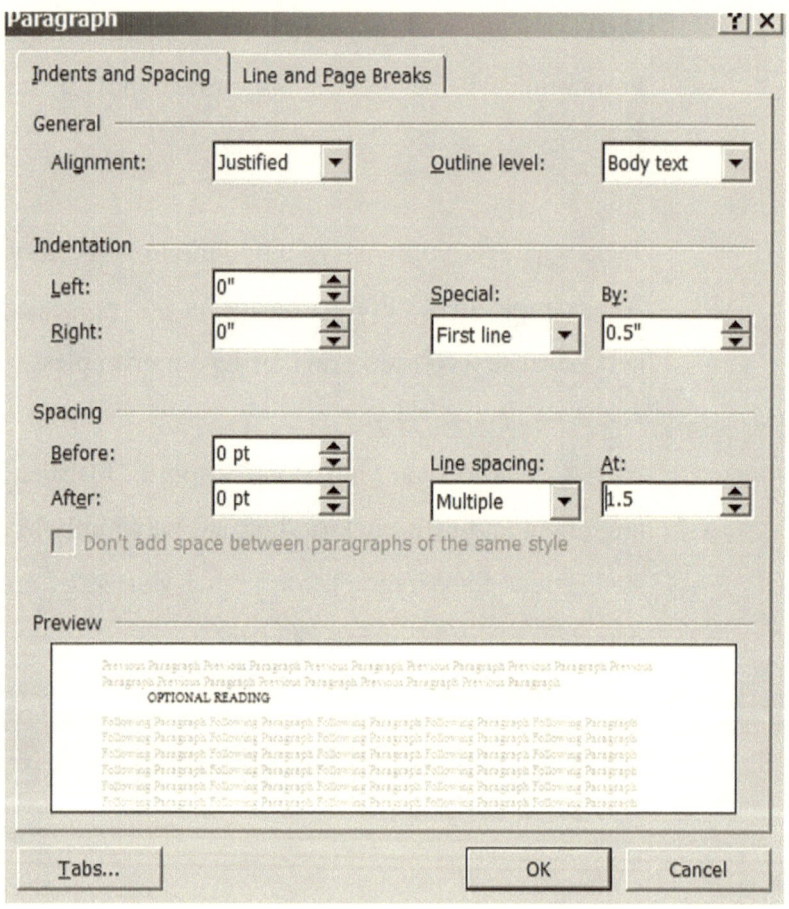

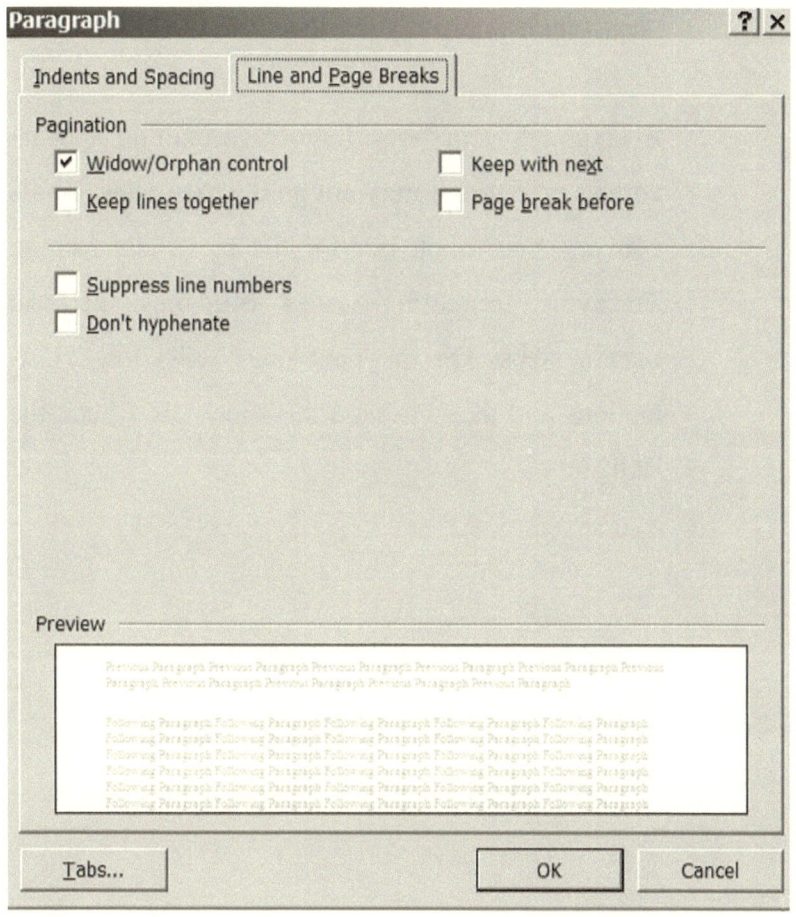

You, however, will be the determiner for how you wish your typed story to appear on each page.

Next step is to proof your book.

Eventhough your book interior formatting appears correct in Word, it may not be the case after Kindle converts your book interior file to Kindle format. To avoid formatting issues you must perform certain steps: On the next page, click on View, Options and then click on the View tab. Check the "All" box:

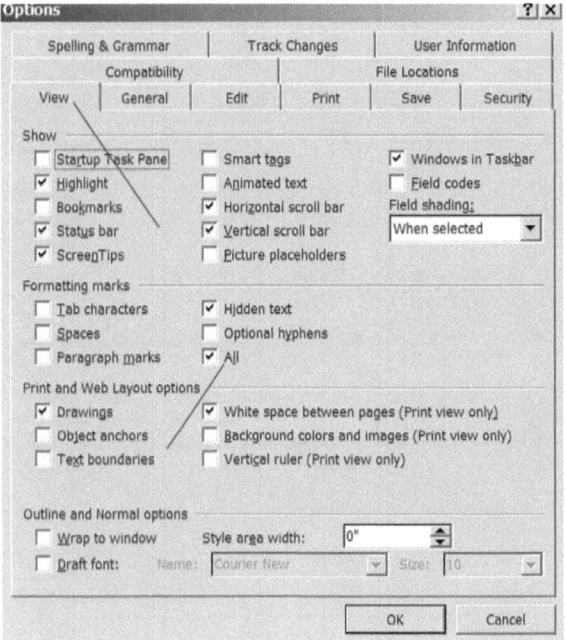

Checking the "All" allows elements not visible in the Word document to appear as artifacts or spaces which will appear as redundant tiny dots the size of periods. Only "superfluous" dots must be deleted. Paragraph header symbols "¶" are also now visible, as in the next example on the following page:

An author attempts to control a reader's attention, also tries to present the story in an understanding way. However, the author cannot over-ride a reader's innate attention span or a reader's comprehension ability. As a reader's eyes come upon each written word they silently speak the word. How the reader articulates their speech "aloud" to the world is how a reader "listens" to his or her self reading.

Next step is to delete every inappropriate dot as pointed to in the previous example. Be certain the ¶ symbols are orderly and aligned vertically by making sure they are properly justified, centered or aligned-left.

Your accuracy determines if all elements of your manuscript will be arranged and formatted correctly on your final product and will pass KDP's quality checks.

Dots are part of any Word document when the "all" box under tools, options, view is checked; so be careful to delete "only" inappropriate dots. Check the entire manuscript for superfluous dots. Afterwards, uncheck the "All" box in tools, options, view to avoid clutter.

The next step is to click on tools, grammar and spelling and then check the entire document for spelling and grammar errors.

Next, select View, normal and then carefully scroll down the document from the beginning. Look for misaligned paragraphs and anything that appears odd.

The next step is to save the manuscript file as both a doc file for E-books and a PDF file for paperback books which is a KDP requirement for paperback manuscripts. Book covers can be JPG for E-books, but book covers must be PDF formatted for paperbacks.

SOME FINAL THOUGHTS ABOUT YOUR
BOOK'S INTERIOR

When writing your story I suggest each written page be visually uncluttered. Avoid excessive quotes, exclamation marks, ornate lead-in paragraph elements or flamboyant chapter ingredients. The strength of your story should stand alone without the need to accessorize it. Placing your name or the title of your book at the head of every page is distracting.

Reader's eyes are used to seeing New Times Roman fonts. Other fonts may interfere with the reading experience. Illustrations are fine for children's books. However, pictures inside a book take away the imagining mood of reader. When describing a scene or a character, use the power of words to titillate a reader's imagination.

BUILDING YOUR BOOK COVERS

Please note: My instructions are for a 6" by 9" paperback with cream colored paper. Mate or glossy book cover is your call; I use either for diversity.

A note about using cream paper versus white paper for your manuscript: I opt to use cream paper for my paperback book manuscripts because I prefer it. Cream paper is thicker than white paper and has a solid tactile feel. All my books are on cream paper. Many book designers prefer white paper because it is believed white paper offers better contrast for illustrations. Some of my books are children's books with multiple illustrations, yet I find cream paper presents illustrations quite well. Moreover; to me, white paper is flimsy to the touch and visually too stark; cream paper offers a visually softer reading experience. Also, turning cream paper pages provides a hefty feel.

The following steps and examples are for you to get a head start in bookcover creation. If you deviate in any way, you may not pass KDP's strict requirements.

Step one: download a 6X9, cream color, 40-page cover template from KDP help-resource page. To get the template, click on "download one of our templates" as shown here:

| Q Topic or Keyword | Search Help |

Prepare, Publish, Promote › Prepare Your Book › Create Your Cover › Paperback Cover Resources

Paperback Cover Resources

We have several resources to help you format your paperback cover. How can we help you?

Give me tools to make it easier

• **Free tool.** For help designing a basic cover that meets KDP specifications, try Cover Creator.
• **Templates.** To create a print-ready paperback cover with programs that can open a PNG or PDF file and save a PDF file, download one of our templates.
• **File setup calculator.** For help calculating your book dimensions, try our calculator.

You will be taken to:

Choose your template

How to use your template

Trim size

1. Open the PDF or PNG file for the Paperback Book Cover Template in your image editing software.

Select an option ⬦

2. Create a new layer in your image editing software. This layer will serve as the design layer.

Page count

3. Design your cover in the design layer, using the template PDF or PNG file as the guide layer. The artwork should extend to the outside edge of the template's pink zone to ensure a white border will not exist within the printed work. Do not move the guide layer, as it is properly aligned for our printing specifications.

Paper color

4. Ensure text and/or images that are intended to be read do not appear in the pink zones of the template.

White ⬦

5. The barcode area is indicated in yellow on the template. Do not place important images or text intended to be read in the barcode location. We suggest filling in this area with your background color or design. KDP will automatically generate a barcode representing your title's ISBN when printing copies of your book.

Download cover template

6. Once your design is complete, you will need to turn off the guide layer so that it is not printed on your final product or rejected during the review process. If you are unable to turn off the guide layer, then you will need to format the artwork so that it completely covers the guide layer.

7. Flatten all layers, save the file as a press quality PDF, and upload the file via KDP.

Select the following options:

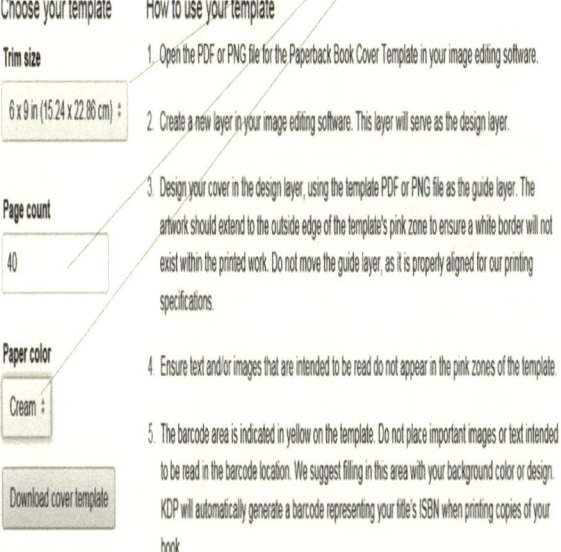

Paperback Cover Templates

These templates help you create print-ready paperback covers with programs like Adobe Photoshop® or Adobe InDesign®. You can use any software that will open a .png or PDF file and save a PDF file.

You'll download these files and submit them to us with exact dimensions, layout, and bleed. There's more information in our Publishing Guidelines.

For best results, we recommend formatting your cover with our templates.

Choose your template

How to use your template

Trim size

6 x 9 in (15.24 x 22.86 cm) ‡

Page count

40

Paper color

Cream ‡

Download cover template

1. Open the PDF or PNG file for the Paperback Book Cover Template in your image editing software.

2. Create a new layer in your image editing software. This layer will serve as the design layer.

3. Design your cover in the design layer, using the template PDF or PNG file as the guide layer. The artwork should extend to the outside edge of the template's pink zone to ensure a white border will not exist within the printed work. Do not move the guide layer, as it is properly aligned for our printing specifications.

4. Ensure text and/or images that are intended to be read do not appear in the pink zones of the template.

5. The barcode area is indicated in yellow on the template. Do not place important images or text intended to be read in the barcode location. We suggest filling in this area with your background color or design. KDP will automatically generate a barcode representing your title's ISBN when printing copies of your book

The downloaded template will be a zip file. After opening the zip, save the PDF file to a folder.

Discard the PNG file. Make sure to "save" the PDF template file to a folder you can remember the name of.

Next step: open the saved PDF file in Photoshop (I shall shorten the name "Photoshop" to PS). Do "not" import the saved PDF template file to PS). It may take a minute or two for rasterizing the template. The template will look like this:

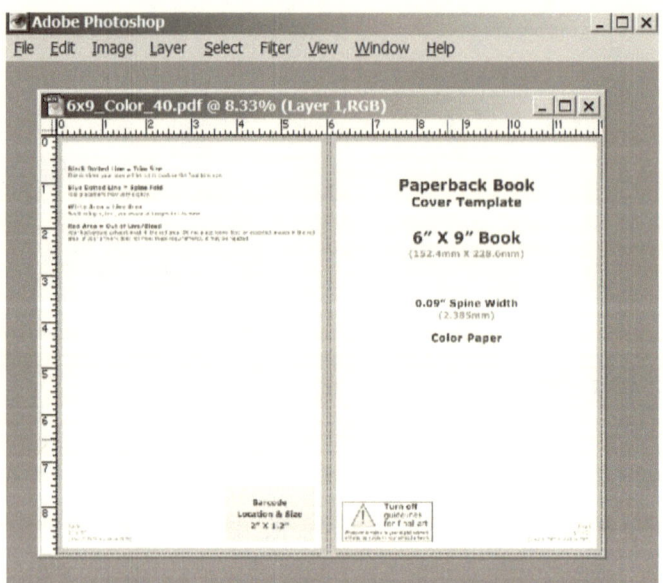

Study this template image carefully. Review what the orange guides and dotted lines all mean in KDP resources. Save the template as a PSD file; you will refer to it later. Move a vertical PS reference guide to the exact center of the template. Move a horizontal PS guide to just above the yellow barcode box. Freely use PS guides to help you align elements on the bookcover once the template lays hidden under your cover illustration creation to prevent overrunning elements onto orange trim guides and spine boundary. You will remove all PS guides from your art work later, before flattening the cover to prepare the PSD cover file for uploading to KDP as a jpeg and PDF file. Flattening your ongoing PSD cover project prematurely removes "all" layers, so do not flatten image until told to later. If you run into trouble, save the PSD file to a jpeg and try to salvage the project, but be aware all PSD layers cannot be altered. PS layers can be complicated but are extremely useful once you understand their usage. Bringing a PSD project back to life after gumming it up requires a learning curve. Deviating from my example PS inputs may cause PS to behave in ways beyond the scope of this primer to explain.

•

Next step: KDP's cover template is a great skeleton for your bookcover. That visual template is derived from the following calculations. The calculations below confirm the accuracy of KDP's template dimensions, spine guides, and trim boundaries to make certain your bookcover and manuscript "will" pass KDP's exacting quality checks:

Add 0.125+0.125+9 (book's initial height). The total: 9.25" will be the final book's height.

Multiply 40 (the page count for this exercise) by 0.0025 (the constant value for cream paper). White paper requires a different constant because white paper is thinner and its lesser bulk affects bookcover dimensions). In this case, the value will be the book's "spine" width: 0.1"

Now add 0.125+0.125+0.1+12(the books initial width). The total: 12.35" will be the books final width for our 40 page "test" book.

While the KDP template is displayed in PS; click Image, image size. The image-tool-box display will look like this:

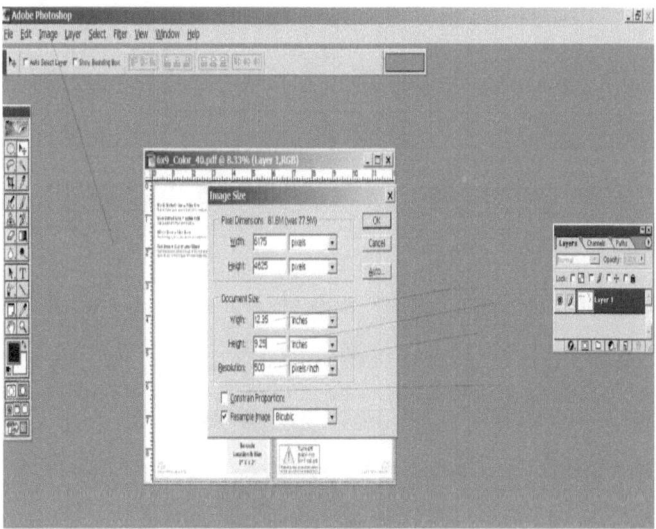

Next step: With the foundation for your book covers in place, you are now ready to build your book covers. Although you can create anything your imagination perceives for your bookcovers, you must be a Photoshop expert to bring exotic illustrations to fruition. However, we are only preparing an elementary bookcover example here. Therefore, I will simplify the bookcover design process.

Using a smartphone, snap a "basic" JPG picture of your backyard, such as the example presented on the following page. Download it to the folder you have been using for all the preceding PS files. Open the picture in PS, so it rests alongside the KDP template. Resize the backyard JPG using PS "Image tool" to match the template image size. In this instance, I did not uncheck the "constrain proportions" in my example image size display box; but it may be necessary for you to precisely line up "your" image in the KDP template boundaries.

The results should appear like this:

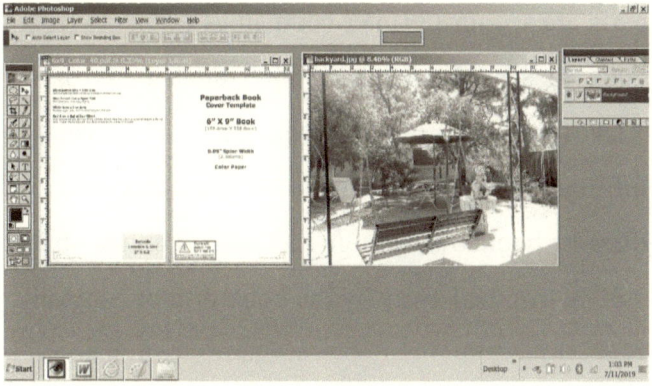

Next step: Carry the PS alignment guides as shown below. As stated earlier; the template orange color parts are sections printer companies utilize to trim a book to size. Remember: the orange parts of the KDP Template are where you are "not" allowed to infringe upon with bookcover elements such as titles or bookcover design elements. Orange spaces will be trimmed away by the book printer company.

Note: Only books with 100 pages or more are allowed to have words such as the name of the author on the spine. Books with less than 100 pages have a too narrow spine for words to fit. Our example book of 40 pages will thus not have a spine with a name. Nevertheless, the orange spine area bordering the spine "cannot" be infringed upon with bookcover design elements.

Photoshop guides should appear as in this image:

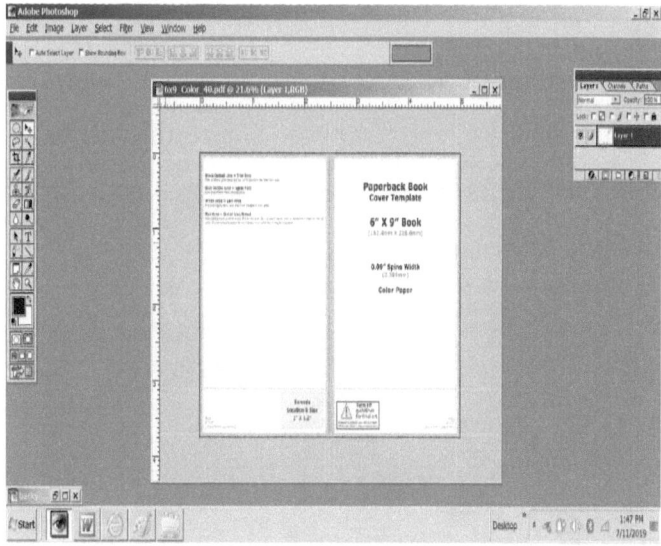

Next step is to "carry" the backyard JPG image onto the template for it to fix exactly over the template. You can place the JPG anywhere on the template, and then move it after placement so it lines up evenly on top of the template. The result will be as follows: Skewing was intentional for this example to fit on this primer page.

If some trim "orange" is showing at the margins, simply "step backward" in PS and resize the backyard JPG image for it to fit exactly on the template. You can also use the PS stamp tool to cover the orange boundary areas if the layer is not locked. If the stamp tool does not function; either save the project as a jpeg and then do a "work around." Or perform a "duplicate" layer which will consume much space to explain here. An image-resize is the ideal solution to fit your jpeg onto the template.

Next step: Type your title and author name using PS type tool. Choose a font such as 48 and bend it then select a color. The results are below: Keep Title outside of PS spine guides and well inside trims.

Note my reference pointers point to Layer tab and the Layers display box.

Next step: Click on Layer tab and select "New layer." Afterwhich a new layer with a number appears in the Layer display box. This new layer will be for the author's name using 18font bold and black color. The results are at pointers:

Next step: Write a brief description of your book in Word to place on the back bookcover (left side of PS project display) then save the PSD file.

Next: click on the PS Type tool and draw the dotted line as in this example. The dotted line will be the boundary for the description you typed to enter inside the dotted box you just drew.

Next step: Open word and highlight-select the description. Paste the description at the upper left hand corner of the dotted line you drew. The results will be:

Next step: Save the PS file as PSD.

Remove all PS guides by sliding horizontal guides up and vertical guides leftward. Afterward; click on Image and then scroll down to "Flatten image." After flattening the image, save the PS file as a PDF for your paperback. Also save the project as jpeg for your E-book. The files are ready to be uploaded to KDP. Your manuscript interior file must be saved as a DOC file and a PDF and then they are ready to be uploaded to KDP.

The process for filling in the spaces presented in KDP Bookshelf for E-book and paperback upload are self-explanatory, so I shall not offer examples. If you become confused at any time; an option in "Help" exists for a support person to immediately call you back via telephone.

DONE, congratulations!

AUDIO BOOKS

The premise of this primer is for building an e-book and a paperback for self-publishing your story. I include this section of audio-books only for informational purpose. Learning and using audio-creation software such as Audacity has a steep learning curve which would require a dedicated book to cover the entire audio-book creation process.

True audio books are narrated by humans. Many people enjoy listening to audio books while driving on road trips or traveling by any mode. Listening to a book being read during commutes makes the passage of time seem to go by quicker.

Other reasons people may enjoy audio books could be because of disabilities or because one's eyes are weary. People could also simply prefer having a book read to them.

Now that you have successfully created your book and it is posted at Amazon for sale as an E-book and paperback, you may desire to also make your book an audio book using ACX and have it listed for sale on Audible. Of course, your E-book is essentially already an audio book because it can be read by wonderful synthesized voices of a Kindle. I regularly listen to the "Sali" voice of my Kindle. For those who do not have a Kindle; Kindle apps are available from Amazon, but those apps are not able to "read" a Kindle e-book file. Only a Kindle device has an option to read a story aloud.

There are work-arounds for a smartphone to read a book aloud, also available software can read books, but those digital voices do not have the "synthesized" quality of a Kindle. Nonetheless, any digital voice cannot mirror a human voice. Only human voices have emotion and can inflect mood into speech. "True" audio books are narrated by humans.

Either you can outsource your book to have a human professional narrator narrate your book; or you can produce and narrate your book yourself which I shall delve into now. Narrating your book is fun.

You must have a sound-proof environment. I used my spacious walk-in closet as my recording studio and left most clothing in the closet to prevent noise from interfering with my narration. After placing a small desk and chair in the closet I employed the following steps:

1. You must control electromagnetic (EM) noise originating from 110V alternating house current. The power supply in a desktop computer running on house current accentuates EM noise. I used my battery operated laptop and connected a 12V laptop power adapter to a Duralast 700peak amp Jump Starter with a cigar lighter receptacle for the 12V laptop power cable to plug into. You can purchase a

laptop 12V adapter specifically designed for your laptop online. A laptop running at full power will drain the built-in laptop battery quickly. Simply plugging your laptop 110V adapter into a wall socket does not eliminate EM.

2. Download the free "Audacity" audio software from the official Audacity website. Audacity worked perfectly for me to narrate two audio books.

3. The following two plug-in files are needed for Audacity: "lame-300.tar.gz" which is a plug-in that encodes MP3 files within Audacity. "Wavestats.ny" is also a necessary analyzer plug-in to assist you with meeting Audible's requirements for keeping an audio file recording within the hertz parameters required by Audible. Audacity's "help and support" pages will help you find those files; even so, those two plug-ins are difficult to find.

4. You will need a microphone. The Marantz Pod Pack 1 worked perfectly for me. It is a cardoid

condenser USB microphone with a snake boom that clamped to my desktop. If you opt to use a different microphone than the one I mentioned (even a balanced one) it may be associated with a preamp or microphone interface, and EM noise may result. I used a Nady SPF-1 pop filter which worked fine. Note that Windows 10 has been reported to have issues with USB microphones, so use Windows 7 (which I did) if you run into problems.

5. All extraneous items that could create noise must be switched off, such as phones, air conditioners, heating furnaces, door bells, and any other noise producing sounds. All human activity happening in your house while you are recording must be halted.

Note: sounds coming from vehicle traffic can be picked up by a recording microphone; even sounds of vehicle tires rolling over tarmac may make its way through the ground and be caught on a recording.

Ground your equipment to "one" water pipe and not to the ground on a house wall electrical receptacle because those wires are bundled inside all house wiring and can be affected by the other wires. Electromagnetic noise is one of the worst enemies of recording, and is difficult to eliminate.

Deviating from my advice may cause your audio recording experience to be quite unpleasant.

BEFORE YOU BEGIN TO RECORD

You should download all "Help" documents ACX-Audible offers and study them. It is essential to also obtain all "Help" documents from Audacity and study them. Watching and listening to Youtube videos relating to narrating and using Audacity shall benefit you greatly. You will of course have to assemble all the Youtube information and weed out useless and incorrect information. Nevertheless, the overall effort is well worth. Some people do post extremely valuable information on Youtube that will assist you in getting your books into Audible.

Once you are operating Audacity with proficiency and are confident your test-recordings will pass Audacity's requirements, you are ready to develop your narrating skills. Here again, Youtube can offer a great deal of wealth toward honing "speaking into a microphone."

Upon pressing the "record" button in Audacity, speaking into a microphone is not as simple as how you may have believed. After you are comfortable with speaking to a microphone you will detect many issues about your speaking voice that require improvement. For example; breathing is a natural phenomenon, but is an issue when recording into a microphone. One cannot stop breathing, but there are things you can do to eliminate sounds coming from inhaling and exhaling.

There are a myriad of other speaking issues regarding narrating, but your ear will develop a keen sense to discover those vocal issues. Once you are able to operate Audacity with precision, it is your speaking voice that will be the most critical element of creating an audiobook. Practice is the only way to become a narrator.

I will be producing a dedicated primer with illustrated examples for audiobook creation soon.

www.ingramcontent.com/pod-product-compliance
Lightning Source LLC
Chambersburg PA
CBHW020350290526
45785CB00005B/2213